THROUGH WOOD

THROUGH WOOD

Alison Swinfen

WILD GOOSE PUBLICATIONS
www.ionabooks.com

Published by
Wild Goose Publications
4th Floor, Savoy House, 140 Sauchiehall St, Glasgow G2 3DH, UK
www.ionabooks.com
Wild Goose Publications is the publishing division of the Iona Community.
Scottish Charity No. SCO03794. Limited Company Reg. No. SCO96243.

ISBN 978-905010-48-6

The publishers gratefully acknowledge the support of the Drummond Trust,
3 Pitt Terrace, Stirling FK8 2EY in producing this book.

A catalogue record for this book is available from the British Library.

Overseas distribution
Australia: Willow Connection Pty Ltd, Unit 4A, 3-9 Kenneth Road,
Manly Vale, NSW 2093
New Zealand: Pleroma, Higginson Street, Otane 4170,
Central Hawkes Bay
Canada: Novalis/Bayard Publishing & Distribution, 10 Lower Spadina Ave.,
Suite 400, Toronto, Ontario M5V 2Z2

Printed on recycled paper by
Thomson Litho, East Kilbride

RECYCLED PAPER

For Richard

ALPHA – OMEGA
AILM – UR

The Gaelic alphabet has 18 letters, each traditionally linked to a tree or shrub, most of which are native to Scotland. Rather like the English tradition of A is for Apple, so in Gaelic A is for Ailm in the ancient Gaelic, 'Leamhan' being the modern rendering: Elm.

In the Iona Community, as part of our common pattern of worship we say a prayer for our own reshaping:

O Christ, the Master Carpenter,
who at the last, through wood and nails,
purchased our whole salvation,
wield well your tools in the workshop of your world,
so that we who come rough-hewn to your bench
may here be fashioned to a truer beauty of your hand.
We ask it for your own name's sake.
Amen

Fashioning wood is at the heart of our practice of faith. It was worked by a surrogate father and lined with cloth by a mother who, casting around in the darkness, settled on a wooden feeding trough to cradle her firstborn son. Jesus, who marks out a pattern for our lives, learned of the grain and the goodness of wood but, having abandoned his day job, sat in wooden boats, cursed a fig tree, walked among olive groves and pointed to a mustard tree as he spoke to people of life in ways they could readily understand. He ended his short life as he had begun it, on wood, hung upon a tree in a place where trees, we may imagine, were clear-felled to make room for the erection of crosses and brutal public execution. He appears again with all the vitality of a garden in full growth, the sap rising once more, the tree of life.

The idea of atonement as a way to grace is not an easy one for us to grasp in our sanitised Christian contexts. The prayer above is marked by the history of the rebuilding of Iona Abbey, by the roots of the Iona Community in the renewal of the common life through a hard common task. We say this prayer and hear from the past the chink of the stonemason's hammer, the sawing of wood, echoes of everyday life at work. We have a certain difficulty in understanding grace in the uneasy theological ideas of salvation purchased 'through wood and nails'. We have learned to be critical, to wonder at such words and concepts. Easier for us is the imagery of coming rough-hewn and of fashioning the self through growth, pruning and the actions over time of work and of worship.

This collection of prayers and poems has its roots in the Gaelic alphabet and in the tradition of understanding Christ as the Alpha and the Omega, the beginning and the end: the Tree of Life. The pieces weave this understanding together with the history, qualities and lore of wood as used in Scotland and across Europe, mindful that most of us today are as dislocated from wood as we are from the land. Our furniture comes flat-packed, to be self-assembled, made from unpoetic materials such as 'chip board' and 'MDF'. These are signs indeed of the technological, bureaucratic, consumer individualism that tears at our social and cultural fabric, and pretends that there is life without history, and without the fashioning and seasoning work of time; that we have progressed beyond the resonant old names given us through wood.

In my experience there is deep, and often justified, suspicion – even hostility – within what I may broadly term the 'green movement' towards the legacies of Christianity. Spirituality may be embraced but her concrete forms of inspiration, the institutions and structures, are often held in contempt. It is for this reason that the poetry and meditations on the lore of wood with which I am working do not seek to sanitise its use or past for the sake of creating a tidy version of one strand of history or another. Baskets are woven of willow. For a poem or a collection to contain this diversity it must work with the warp and the weft, it must know the wood's grain.

And so it is that the traditions of a wood's use, its place in the imagination, and the lore and expressions of religion, pagan and Christian, in Scotland have drawn me to think hard on the relations we have had with wood, with wood's uses and with the uses of poetry in helping us to reforest our imagination. The philosopher Heidegger maintains that, 'The speech of genuine thinking is by nature poetic. The voice of thought must be poetic, because poetry is the saying of truth, the saying of the un-concealedness of being.' (Heidegger 1971:72)

In the flat-pack world of MDF and cheap, stripped pine, the world where taste has been democratised and standardised at the expense of beauty, time, craft and wisdom, poetry is one of the resources we have which may 'unconceal our being'. Poetry can chisel out cracks in language and show glimpses of other worlds. Poetry can bring us into a fresh relationship with the names and sounds and uses of wood. Poetry can reforest our imagination with different ways of speaking about wood. Such poetic activism is often at variance with the safer, un-poetic speech of our mass-produced, wood chip environments. It is a more vulnerable mode of speech, keen to be heard, keen in its content, creative in the craft of dialogue with wood and trees where poetry may begin to occur.

'The form of the poem [...] is crucial to poetry's power to do the things which will always be to poetry's credit: the power to persuade that vulnerable part of our consciousness of its rightness in spite of the evidence of wrongness all around it, the power to remind us that we are hunters and gatherers of values.' (Heaney 1998:467)

'Everything,' says Charles Peguy, 'begins in mysticism and ends in politics' (1943:109). Even greater than the need to speak with wood, through the mysticism of poetry and lore, is the need to speak for wood and for a renewed politics of foresting and the human ecologies, histories and lores that this sustains in the world. In an age where wood is vulnerable and where we speak not of the Caledonian Forest but of reforesting, we need to express wood's vulnerability. We need to speak with it and to it and for its needs, and to use language which accords with its place, here and now.

Across the Highlands of Scotland we see official signposts in dual languages. The English is the 'normal', dominant script, the Gaelic is italicised. In guidebooks to the Scottish mountains we find the same trend. The Irish scholar Marian nic Oin, has described this experience of Gaelic literacy as one of living in a speckled land:

> Taím ag taisteal trén taisteal trén bhfearann breac
> is tá dhá ainm ar gach aon bhaile ann
> *(I am travelling through the speckled land*
> *and every town there has two names)*

Many of these 'speckled' italicised names are ones which hold within them the words for wood. Consider Sail Chaorainn in Glen Shiel, rendered in the guidebooks as 'heel or hill of the rowan', or linger over Scotland's Ordnance Survey maps and search out the names of trees and shrubs in the Gaelic place names which, mercifully, did not suffer the same colonising fate as those of Ireland.

In recognition of the damage done by invading languages, I have reversed this trend, holding the ancient Gaelic letters straight and italicising the English. Colonising, be it through politics, nature, culture or language, takes over space. This is not a simple process, but is freighted with problems, producing often painful yet sometimes beautiful, life-giving yet deeply paradoxical results. Poetic activism by language activists has brought some justice to those who have been dislocated from their language, as well as from their land.

Through wood…

THE CHAPEL

This is a place
for the gnarled and
the knotted, the
chiselled, and sawn and
chipped.

And into this place
come the broken
and burnt,
the charred,
the rough hewn
and chopped.

And in this place
there is shaping
and honing, a
planed-piece, a
turning and a twist.

Where the deep root
meets the strong branch
and the bark crosses silver
the kindling brings a
bright light
that bursts.

ALPHABET

There are several different versions of the tree alphabet. Each letter here has the ancient Gaelic, its modern equivalent and the English name for the tree.

LETTER	ANCIENT	MODERN	ENGLISH
A	ailm	leamhan	wych elm
B	beith	beithe	birch
C	coll	calltainn	hazel
D	dair	darach	oak
E	eadha	critheann	aspen
F	feàrn	feàrna	alder
G	gort	eidheann	ivy
H	uath	sgitheach	hawthorn
I	iogh	iubhar	yew
L	luis	caorann	rowan
M	muin	fìonan	vine
N	nuin	uinnseann	ash
O	onn	conasg	gorse
P	peith bhog	beithe	birch/downy birk/ guelder rose
R	ruis	droman	elder
S	suil	seileach	willow
T	tinne	cuileann	holly
U	ur	iubhar/ fraoch	yew/heather

Elm is renowned for its strength and beauty and has been used to make furniture, ships and water pipes. Its leaves were used in animal fodder, being rich in nutrients and proteins. The burr elm is particularly prized for furniture-making because of the patterns made by a viral infection which show in spalted timber.

Elm was traditionally used for coffins but in Scotland was not thought of as a mystical tree. In Greek myth an elm grove sprang up when Orpheus returned after his fateful journey to the underworld to play music that would mourn Euridyce.

Today the mourning for the elm continues in England and increasingly in Scotland as the species is killed by Dutch Elm disease.

DELIGHT

I cannot help it.
This world delights
me. I know
I should dig around
in peat bogs for insight
or ironise the life
out of all and sundry;
cautious, careful, critical,
pacing the poetry
until it is flattened
to prose.

Even in the
bare purple of
a wych elm
in midwinter
mourning
I can
hear the sap
rising again
to meet me
with my name.

The wind can have my caution.

The first birches in Scotland have been dated to around 6,000 BC. A coarse-grained, whitish wood, birch rots rapidly in contact with the earth and little distinction can be made between the heartwood and the sapwood. It has been used for herring barrels, clogs, and bobbins and reels for spinning, as well as for flooring and plywood. The backpack of Ötzi the Ice Man (Europe's oldest natural human mummy) was made of birch wood.

Birch burns with a clear flame and is therefore also used for malt drying, and whisky and kipper smoking. It is an emblem of Russia where birch twigs have been used in saunas to beat the naked body to stimulate circulation and increase vitality. It is a graceful, pioneer species, the first to colonise and produce new growth after the retreating ice sheets of the ice age, rendering upper moorland areas fertile.

Named after Brigid, the Irish white goddess, for the whiteness of its bark, birch was also considered to bring poetic gifts, to nourish and nurture. Birch twigs were used traditionally to light the Beltane fires of May. As Christianity crept in under the cover of earlier festivals, the Beltane tradition of a day's release from marriage vows under the birches was replaced by that of dancing around a maypole of birch on the village green. At the winter solstice and Hogmanay it was a birch broom that brushed out the New Year ready for the light and for the new.

NAKED WRITING

And then the
writing took me,
as the wind
that took the
bright golden leaves
from the birch
tree
last night.

Exposed,
naked
against the
white sky
of the page,
and as bare as
the twigs
that are
my words,
standing
appalled and
defiant
against the
winter to
come,
when all
will be taken
from me,
and celebrated,
and consumed.

The long, straight growth of coppiced hazel made it ideal for huts, hurdles, creels and fish weirs. Hazel is also the traditional wood used for water divining. In the Gaelic traditions the poetic arts have a long association with the hazel, which was considered a tree of knowledge. Autumn babies were fed on the fluid from unripe hazel nuts so that they might develop the gift of second sight and prophetic powers. When the moon was waning, hazel wood was believed to grow brittle.

OR PERHAPS...

Or perhaps you
are a robin,
turmoil
seeping from
the wound
in your breast,
silvered,
with a fierce
honour,
tempting me,
taunting me,
as close
as my gasp at
the nearness of
your loveliness,
then, a blur of feathers,
a shaking of the
brittle
hazel branch,
and all I have is
a scattering of raindrops,
lighting my skin.

There are bright territories
in your eye.

It is a forbidding
song.

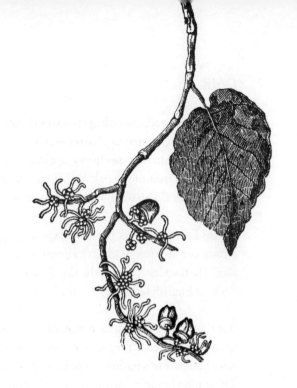

Often long-lived, the oak gives a wood that is hard and strong, ideal for shipbuilding, furniture, panelling, barrel-making. Since the iron age it has been used as the principal timber in dwellings because of its immense durability and resilience. Acorns, the fruit of the oak, were important fodder for pigs and, when roasted, for people. Oak is also used in tanning leather.

Across Europe the oak has been experienced in faith practices as a mystical tree. Its strong conduction of electrical current linked it to the weather gods, and it was sacred to the Celtic god of the sky, Taranis. Thunder also linked the oak to war, great fleets of English battleships being built of its timbers.

But the oak is a peaceable, hospitable tree, offering shelter to hundreds of different species and often acting as host to the mistletoe. At Rogationtide, the fifth Sunday after Easter, it was traditional to beat the parish bounds, which were marked by oaks. These trees became known as Gospel Oaks when used as preaching crosses.

In early August the oak produces new shoots known as Lammas shoots, from the Christian festival of Lammas, itself based on the Celtic festival of Lùnasdal. Yuletide, at the winter solstice, brought the tradition of burning great logs of oak, in honour of the Viking god of thunder, Thor.

SHELTER

And I wish you
wood smoke
curling round the pole star
and sundials
that count
stories.

And I desire
peace for
you,
ochre and orange,
resting in
the warm light
of candles
on oak wood.

And I will be
still for you,
stained light
and shadows,
smoothing your
name in the
swell of the sea.

EADHA   *Aspen*

A supple wood, bending easily into barrels, cutting well but providing little heat when burning. The aspen today is predominantly used in the match industry. It was known as the 'quaking tree' because of the way its leaves tremble, and sometimes it was also called 'old wives' tongues'.

It is one of the trees traditionally thought to have provided the wood for the crucifixion and, for this reason, the aspen at the head of Loch Shiel was 'dressed down' on Good Friday

TREMBLING

The leaves of the aspen tremble
on the islands they say
it is with shame.

At the Loch head
they gather
a tide mark of aches
and grumbles
and gossiping pains.

Their words scold,
blunt, slimy
seaweed-cold.

Carving
a curse against the dark
their bite is worse
by far
than their bark.

He bows out
of their merriment.

Spent.

The tide turns
and silence
cracks the salty
air.

They return searching
the beach at dawn,
combing the tangled
shavings into
stories and sense.

They tell of a
supple body
bending,
a quaking,
of spilt wine.

FEARN

Alder

Light, durable, stronger if submerged in water for long periods and therefore used in barrels, as well as for housing timbers and ploughs. It was traditionally used for making the highland harp. In times of war, it was a key component in the manufacture of gunpowder.

Its beauty, particularly when turned, gave it the name 'Scottish mahogany'.

COVENTRY

You sent me there against my will.

I wanted to talk.

To you.

I found charred alder,
blackened candlesticks,
on a cold altar
in the rubble of chanting words.
Crossed and quiet,
the remains of a strong
fire, compelling
more
than rest
from war.

Evergreen, defying the harsh winter. Its glossy leaves make it a sign of luck and wealth. In Roman mythology it was a symbol of friendship, of Bacchus. In Christianity its associations are with everlasting life. Its clinging habit speaks of faithfulness, but also of the need for discipline, pruning, control. Largely its uses are decorative. Its heart-wood is ivory in colour.

THE YEAR

The year turned
first refracting the light
through the
rain into
a taut bow.

Then twisting like
ivy round a tree trunk
spinning it like
a whip and top

turning,

       turning

until it would

topple
       and

       drop.

A leaf,
       wind-flipped.

Oak gall on its
underside,
the brown larvae
in the bowls
of the bole,
of the year.

And everywhere,
a green music of
life coursing in vein,

coursing though field

dripping, filling,
overflowing,
into full flood.

Tough and fine-grained hawthorn burns well even when the wood is green. It is a particularly durable wood, making it ideal for cogs and wheels and milling. A traditional boundary marker, it was planted to create thousands of miles of hedges during the enclosures.

Hawthorn has a history of medical use to stimulate blood circulation and as a tonic after the winter. Blossoming in the spring, and with its early leaves bringing some of the first fresh green food to the table, symbolism associated with hawthorn is of overflowing abundance, of fecundity. It was the tree dedicated to Hera, the Roman goddess of childbirth. A heavy crop of berries in the autumn is said to signal a hard winter to come.

In folklore the hawthorn provided a trysting place for fairies, and people took care to be respectful towards it.

JAZZ FISHING

It was the dead of winter
when we sent him back
to the earth. A Viking
he left the room, dressed
for the Assynt hills, dancing
through fire to John Coltrane.

In his breast pocket, a
shiny conker, brown
as trout, planted for
the green days of spring.

In the rich, loamy soil
of his heart,
we knew a great
chestnut would grow.

A sharp morning,
on the Aultbea shore
he stands now,
a fine line tugs the
fish as they
flash through
the new sunlit air.

The old paper,
an Tir, an Canan, 'sna daoine,
kindles a small fire.

He stokes it with
hawthorn, green
from the solitary
tree.

He knows the way
from white May
to red October,
and the fiercest blaze

Waking from dreams
with our nets empty
we find him
in the smoke
of the dawn
turning a full catch of
fresh speckled fish
over the fire
on the lochan beach,

This is the start of
a great northern feast.

A most venerated tree, hollowing out to give stability and durability often over hundreds of years, and regenerating from below. The ability of yew poles to outlast those made of iron led to its being called 'iron wood'. It was used to make longbows and was planted in churchyards, ostensibly to prevent cattle from eating it and being poisoned. Burnt for ashes on Ash Wednesday, it is associated with death but is also a symbol of resurrection at Easter.

The wood is resilient, with a beautiful grain and colour; it is resistant to rot and damp and makes fine turned objects.

The ancient name for Ireland, Ierne, meant 'yew island'. In Norse mythology Odin hung upside down in the Nordic Tree of Life, known as Yggdrasil, for nine days. The Yggdrasil is often interpreted to have been a yew tree and from it Odin brought back runes for an alphabet.

The Celtic calendar connects the yew to the festival Samhain, and with it to All Saints' Day, where the yew stands guard at the doorway between the living and the dead, which, it was believed, was opened at this time.

THE NIGHT STAIR

A silence like no other
is ne'r day in the
morning. The world is
sleeping off the ill
effects of the
old year and
it is too soon to
speak any
story into the new.

Quiet as thick
flakes of snow. Quiet
as the rising and falling
of a child's sleep. Quiet
as the sleep of
the dead,
under the yew.

Quiet
as the abbey church at
candlefall when
Amens are said,
and on the air,
before the latch drops,
behind the night stair,
the last echo of God
breathing in our
prayer.

Rowan is a hard and heavy wood, used for spinning wheels, flooring, oars, hoops and herring barrels. It also makes excellent charcoal when burnt.

It too has mystical associations and was thought to have the power to expel evil. The Celtic goddess Brigid (the Christian St Bride) is associated with the rowan and she is also the patron saint of spinning. Consequently rowan was literally woven into housing and at Lammas rowan wood crosses were hung over lintels.

In Scottish tradition it was unlucky to cut the rowan unless it was to be used for festive purposes. Its English name is of Norse origin, *runa*, meaning 'secret' or 'whisper'.

YOUR NAME

I kept your name alive.
I spoke it to the rowan
and the rain, to the river too.
I crossed the city and
we conversed. Strangers
would see me smile, would
recognise your presence
in the curving of my lips.

Sometimes I would reel
at the shock of it.
Not a name
to conjure with lightly.
I'd throw it into the sky, a bright
blazing torch, and,
wrong-footed by
the warmth of it passing
through the air,
I'd reach into the flame
for balance,

and burn.

Not a native of the North, the vine is strong in biblical tradition. The scouts returning from Canaan, the Promised Land, brought huge grapes back with them as they told of the land of milk and honey. Noah was the first mentioned in the Bible to plant a vineyard.

'I am the vine and you are the branches.' 'Drink all of this, it is my blood.' The sayings of Jesus point perhaps most strongly to the life-giving qualities of the wine as blood, and the vine as the image of life, growth, vigour.

PASSION'S FLOWERS

That night
we ate of the
fish of the sea
and we heard
sadness sing to us
in blood
and in wine.

Now, I do not know your
name, but your
hands are rough
from the earth
there are thorns
in your flesh, and
you walk
on the dew
of the day.

I do not know the story
but the lines around
your waking eyes
tell of a journey
into life, and
there is mischief
in those outstretched
hands, which fear
my touch.

But this I know,
this:
we meet here, where
the face of death
rises into laughter,
and calls out my name
among the deep,
rambling purple
where passion flowers.

NUIN   *Ash*

The ash is a durable wood and thus has been used for tools, utensils, coarser furniture, ploughs, carts and wheels. Shinty sticks are also often made of it. It burns well when fresh and is light in colour with a dark heartwood. Best crafted when green, the wood will tighten as it dries.

The Norse tree Yggdrasil, as well as being thought of as a yew, is also reputed to have been an ash tree, linking heaven and hell. The representations of the Green Man, a sign of fertility in folklore, show the figure decked in ash.

Ash sap was fed to newborns so that the magic force of the gods would be transferred to them.

With the oak, the ash is a seasonal weather-vane.

AFTER THE FLOOD

Ash before the oak
in fifty-three years
never such a soak.

The river
exhausted from
days of turning the
land through the
mangle,
hung itself out
in the trees
to dry.

The trees
those left
standing at the end of
the spin cycle
welcomed the twigs
and the green
weed now pegged
out on their
bare branches.

And nestling in their
roots, rocks, and
bright frosted pebbles
the river bed freshly made.

In the field, a
high water mark
of blood-red beech leaves
dyes the skin of a
clean earth.

It is a good drying day.

Gorse was the fuel for the poor; it was also cattle fodder and of great practical use for sweeping chimneys, dyeing, filling drains, laying path foundations, cleaning wells, and for roofing and fencing.

It was reputed to make a poor gift as it would result in quarrels, but there is also a saying, 'When gorse is out of flower, then kissing is out of fashion', which grew out of its enduring blossoms.

If stuck into the roof on a May morning, it would herald the summer and bring luck.

KISSING

With you
kissing is
never out of
fashion.

The last time
we stood in
this garden
it left wounds
in your hands
and your side.

So I will not ask to
touch you.

There are thorns still
in your flesh.

Already you
wear gorse gold

but still, like Midas,
I hunger to have
and to hold.

PEITHE

Guelder Rose / Downy Birk

Found in hedgerows across the North, the guelder rose's white flowers come heavy with fragrance. It grows best in damp climates and produces a fine display of red-orange berries in the autumn. An older name for the guelder rose was water- or swamp-elder because its berries look similar to elderberries.

The guelder rose bark has medicinal uses; it can be made into a tincture for treating cramps.

MIDWINTER SPRING

Is this midwinter spring?

Low light and candle flame
jasmine and holly,
and guelder roses
in pregnant ground?

Outside incense rises.
The light above is as soft
as a cradle of hay,
creamy as sheepskin
to the tiny clutch.

Inside life tears at the
incomprehending
darkness, bleeding
its way
into the world.
Crying out
at the precision
that flays flesh
from bone,
she breathes
him out

peithe

for a thorny world.

Elder wood, if cut in winter when the sap is at its lowest, makes excellent reeds for piping, creating a sweeter and louder sound than those cut from cane. The flowers and berries of the elder can be made into juice and drinks. It produces little heat when burnt.

Judas hung himself on an elder, and it is another tree traditionally thought to have been used for the crucifixion. The berries make 'blood'. These associations with violent death may also have led to the belief that elder wood was a bad wood for a baby's cradle.

THE CRADLE

She laid him
on elder wood
wrapped him in
the down of birk
and wove a cradle
with willow.

Not a good wood
said the First,
a hard wood
said the Second
oh but
a true wood
said the Third.

SUIL

The willow is tough, pliable, strong and ideal for fencing, basketry and building coracles. Its associations are with rivers and summertime.

Willow has long been linked with the moon and with the feminine. It was sacred to poets and provided wood for the harp. Beltane, the Celtic festival of the sun god Belin in May, derived its name from Bel, the Sumerian god of willows.

SUIL – WILLOW

For children
you come as spring
soft, furry and grey
as kittens, then
gambolling in the
early warmth
of the wind,
as minty as
a lamb.

For us, though
you come as summer
tough, strong, bent
into a basket for Moses
a strong oar dipping like oil
into the troubled waters.
A scar on your
back from the
crack of the whip.
Shafted.

You bend to draw
patterns in
the earth, to taste the
lake, to tickle the trout
and then
after the whipping
the weeping,
the bleeding
and the stripping
you come as the dance
plucking the leaves
one by one from
the willow tree.

TINNE   *Holly*

A dense and fine-grained wood, beautiful when turned and inlaid, and used in printing blocks and for mathematical instruments, as well as for whip shafts. When burnt it generates a fierce heat.

As with the rowan, it was said to be unlucky to cut down a holly tree. The water collected in its leaves was believed to be holy and was sprinkled as a blessing on newborns.

HOLY

Hard, heavy
honey-black,
you measure out
time,
measure out the autumn
and spring,
mathematical,
arithmetical
marking out the
integers of seconds,
marking the
movement of space.

Evergreen, you
are for all
seasons, your work
never done.

You hold out
your thorny hands
and gather the rain,

holy water

for
sprinkling over
the newborn,

for
sprinkling over the dead.

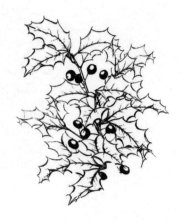

YOUR NAME

I kept your name alive.

I spoke it to the yew,
to the yearning
to the graveyard too.

Older now,
I knelt among the ashes
where the dead
fire breathes.

Never a name
to conjure with,
lightly.

Not a name to catch
in a flame.

Like a crossed bow
arching in anguish,
quivering in
the cruelty of the

green city air,

I finger the
blackening
bone-grey
of the burning,

And watch for
the silver
streaking
my prayer.

MY NAME, *TOO*

I have
written
tunes
for you.

The first,
a wild jig
in A.
Wheeling and
whirling,
breathless
with danger.

The rowan
brought me
little protection,
though it
burns with
a bright
hot flame.

The second,
a lament
in G minor,
sung softly
among the ashes,
as you skipped away.

And there was no dancing.

Under the yew.

Diminuendo.

Nothing grew.

Midwinter.
The sap, low.

An air, rising.

Behind me,
a twig cracks.

You take a
sharp knife
to the elder.
Fashion
a new reed.

On the
count of three,
you pipe
my name.

This time there is
no heat or burning.

This time I know
not to touch the flame.

ACKNOWLEDGEMENTS

I thank
the whisper
of oak,
the rowan blood,
the field
the folk
the violets
which grow
in the litter
and mould.

I sing
of the lovely
shapes
of branches
and trunks
and crowns
bending
and waving,

weaving
with words
through
the leaves
that live
which turn
the phrase,
like
a bowl
on a lathe.

Through wood.

Thanks to Gearoid Denvir, Janet Macdonald for things Gaelic; Anne Phipps – for seeing through the words to the comma, the intimacy, the dance and the dot; Roy Phipps for teaching me to know and love trees; Lesley Saunders, Joy Mead, Robert Swinfen and Kathy Galloway, for belief; Sandra Kramer and Neil Paynter for seeing the wood for the trees.

REFERENCES

Heaney, S., 1998, 'Crediting Poetry: The Nobel Lecture 1995', in *Opened Ground*, Faber and Faber, ed., London, pp. 446–467.

Heidegger, M., 1971, *Poetry, Language, Thought*, Harper Colophon Books, New York.

Peguy, C., 1943, *Basic Verities*, trans. Ann and Julian Green. Pantheon Books, New York.

For a wonderful example of a community Gaelic lore and language project involving wood and the old Gaelic names see the Gaelic-English bilingual publication: a' chraobh *the tree*, Dornoch Studio 2000, Sutherland, Scotland.

The feast of information, lovingly presented, that is *Flora Celtica* provided much inspiration: Milliken, W. & Bridgewater, S., 2004, *Flora Celtica: Plants and People in Scotland*. Birlinn, Edinburgh.

Hageneder, F., 2005, *The Living Wisdom of Trees*. Duncan Baird Publishing, Edinburgh.

My preferred field guide is: Sterry, P., 2007, *Collins Complete British Trees*. Collins, London.

Trees for Life have a website which is an ever-expanding treasure trove of tree-lore, tree-justice and activism: http://www.treesforlife.org.uk/

THE AUTHOR

Alison Swinfen lives and works in Glasgow and is a member of the Iona Community. She is Professor of Languages and Intercultural Studies in the Faculty of Education at the University of Glasgow where she is Director of the Centre for Studies in Faith, Culture and Education.

Wild Goose Publications is the publishing house of the Iona Community, which is:

- An ecumenical movement of men and women from different walks of life and different traditions in the Christian church
- Committed to the gospel of Jesus Christ, and to following where that leads, even into the unknown
- Engaged together, and with people of goodwill across the world, in acting, reflecting and praying for justice, peace and the integrity of creation
- Convinced that the inclusive community it seeks must be embodied in the community it practises

Together with its staff, the community is responsible for:
- The islands residential centres of Iona Abbey, the MacLeod Centre on Iona, and Camas Adventure Centre on the Ross of Mull

and in Glasgow:
- The administration of the Community
- Work with young people
- A publishing house, Wild Goose Publications
- Its association in the revitalising of worship with the Wild Goose Resource Group

The Iona Community was founded in Glasgow in 1938 by George MacLeod, minister, visionary and prophetic witness for peace, in the context of the poverty and despair of the Depression. Its original task of rebuilding the monastic ruins of Iona Abbey became a sign of hopeful rebuilding of community in Scotland and beyond. Today, it consists of about 280 Members, mostly in Britain, and 1500 Associate Members, with 1400 Friends worldwide. Together and apart, the community 'follows the light it has, and prays for more light'.

For information on the Iona Community contact:
The Iona Community, Fourth Floor, Savoy House,
140 Sauchiehall Street, Glasgow G2 3DH, UK.
Phone: 0141 332 6343
e-mail: admin@iona.org.uk; web: www.iona.org.uk

For enquiries about visiting Iona, please contact:
Iona Abbey, Isle of Iona, Argyll PA76 6SN, UK.
Phone: 01681 700404

For books, CDs & digital downloads published by Wild Goose Publications:
www.ionabooks.com